Essentials
of *River Kayaking*

by the American Canoe Association

American
Canoe
Association

A book of this sort presents not the opinions of one person but rather the distilled wisdom and experience of many. Accordingly, in compiling it, we have benefited greatly from the ideas and suggestions of others. These debts are simply too numerous to name in full, so we resort to thanking only those whose services were especially noteworthy. Charlie Wilson and Patty Caruthers helped identify a need for this book and encouraged us to write it. Becky Molina and Mike Aronoff were helpful and generous reviewers whose suggestions made the text more clear and accurate. The book as a whole owes much to an American Canoe Association (ACA) textbook compiled by Pam Dillon. Dillon's work, in turn, owes much to Tom Foster's earlier writings. Russell Helms has been enormously dedicated and good humored in seeing this book through the publication process, and without his expertise the whole venture would have foundered long ago. Others who have contributed include Sam Fowlkes, Bruce Lessels, Kent Ford, Greg Wolfe, and Kim Whitley. Alabama Small Boats provided significant material support. The Standards Committee of the Safety Education and Instruction Council reviewed the manuscript, offered valuable suggestions, and endorsed the book for use with ACA courses. To those other individuals who contributed their comments and their energies and who are not singled out here, we express our sincere gratitude.

Published by Menasha Ridge Press
First edition, first printing

Text and cover design by Travis Bryant
Illustration on page 35 by Les Fry (updated for this book by Scott McGrew). Illustrations on pages 29–33 are from previous American Canoe Association publications and are by Carol A. Moore. All other illustrations are by Travis Bryant and Scott McGrew.

Library of Congress Cataloging-in-Publication Data
Essentials of river kayaking/by the American Canoe Association.
p. cm.
ISBN 0-89732-586-9
1. Kayaking. I. American Canoe Association.

GV783.E77 2004
797.122′4—dc22

2004049887
CIP

Disclaimer: Outdoor activities are an assumed risk sport. This book cannot take the place of appropriate instruction for paddling, swimming, or lifesaving techniques. Every effort has been made to make this guide as accurate as possible, but it is the ultimate responsibility of the paddler to judge his or her ability and act accordingly.

Menasha Ridge Press
2204 First Avenue South, Suite 102
Birmingham, AL 35233
(205) 322-0439
www.menasharidge.com

American Canoe Association
7432 Alban Station Road, Suite B-232
Springfield, VA 22150-2311
(703) 451-0141
www.acanet.org

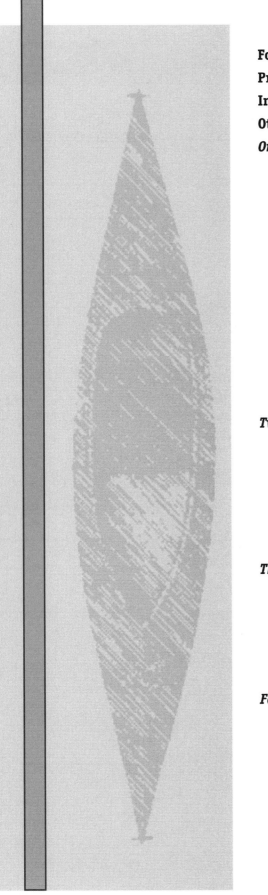

The ACA works to promote the safety and enjoyment of all paddlers, in any type of boat, and on any type of water environment. Founded in 1880, the ACA is working toward its third century of actively promoting paddlesports across the United States, providing programs and services to its members and the American public.

The mission of the American Canoe Association (ACA) is to promote the health, social, and personal benefits of canoeing, kayaking, and rafting, and to serve the needs of all paddlers for safe, enjoyable paddling opportunities.

Safe, enjoyable paddling requires knowledge and skill, and *Essentials of River Kayaking* will help you gain both. In fact, the best way to enjoy paddling a kayak is to develop kayaking skills with safety in mind.

In addition to reading this manual and practicing what you learn from it, we strongly recommend formal instruction. The American Canoe Association's courses emphasize safety, enjoyment, and skills development. Greater skills lead to greater fun and the ability to progress confidently to the next level of enjoyment. With that in mind, I invite you to become a member of the American Canoe Association, the nation's recognized leader in the field of paddlesport instruction.

We hope that *Essentials of River Kayaking* assists you in advancing your personal paddling goals.

Happy kayaking!

Pamela S. Dillon, Executive Director

American Canoe Association
7432 Alban Station Boulevard, Suite B-232
Springfield, VA 22150
(703) 451-0141
www.acanet.org

Course Goals

AMERICAN CANOE ASSOCIATION

ESSENTIALS OF RIVER KAYAKING

Safety: To safely paddle on rivers up through Class I, perform self rescue, and respond to emergencies that arise.

Enjoyment: To become aware of paddling opportunities and the rewards of lifetime participation in paddling.

Skills: To acquire the ability to safely and enjoyably paddle on Class I rivers.

Preface

Paddling is a wonderful, diverse sport that appeals to a broad spectrum of American society. Kayaking is the fastest-growing discipline within paddling, with an increase in participation of over 182% from 1995 through 2002. In fact, kayaking is the fastest growing outdoor sport of any kind. While sea kayaking and whitewater kayaking garner most of the media's attention, most new paddlers enter the sport through "recreational kayaking." These beginning paddlers want to paddle on easy rivers and less-exposed coastal areas, as well as lakes, ponds, and swamps. The rewards of recreational kayaking are numerous, but while recreational kayaking is less risky than whitewater or serious sea kayaking, hazards do exist. Learning only from your mistakes can be a painful process, and there are much better ways of safely learning how to paddle. This book is intended to help the novice gain useful skills and knowledge, so that river kayaking can be enjoyed in a safe, pleasurable manner. The ideas and tips expressed here represent the collective wisdom of literally thousands of instructors who have tested and tried these techniques on thousands of rivers, lakes, and streams. We hope they will be as helpful to you as they have been to the many others who have gotten hooked on this beautiful, challenging sport.

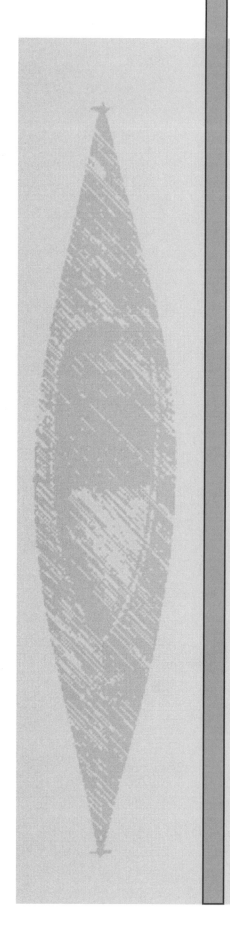

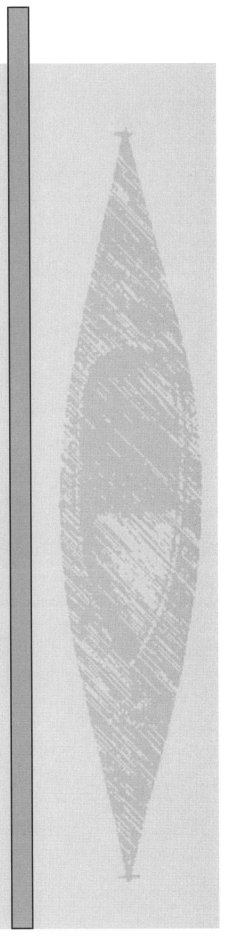

Introduction

Safe paddling requires, above all, the exercise of good judgment. Good judgment means understanding the challenges and hazards inherent to any situation and being able to meet them. In recreational kayaking, good judgment means understanding multiple aspects of the sport.

Essentials of River Kayaking provides you with the information and skills needed to make those all-important judgment calls. Beginning with a chapter on gear and risk management, this manual guides you through the major facets of recreational kayaking on rivers: boat terms, trip planning, stroke technique, safety and rescue, and much more. Each chapter contains detailed illustrations that enable understanding of the concepts presented, and review questions that reinforce crucial information and help identify areas needing further study.

Ideally, this book should be considered part of an educational process that includes formal instruction. Lessons from a certified instructor are important. They will help you safely enjoy the sport and start you on the path to being able to exercise good judgment. After your lessons, join a group of knowledgeable, experienced, sensible paddlers. Remember, too, that mastering one aspect of paddling, such as recreational kayaking, does not automatically prepare you for the next one. Venues such as whitewater and open-ocean conditions require special equipment and skills. The transition from a gentle river to whitewater, or from a protected back bay to exposed open water can be difficult and can increase the risk of injury.

There is a wide spectrum of paddlers, ranging from those who enjoy quiet scenery to those who want extreme challenges. The goal for each of us is to identify where on this spectrum we fall and to learn and exercise the appropriate skills to be safe and have fun.

Gordon Black,
Director of Safety Education and Instruction
American Canoe Association

Other Resource Organizations

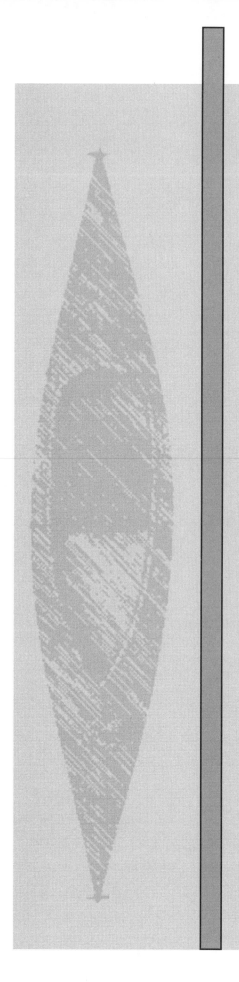

America Outdoors
P.O. Box 10847
Knoxville, TN 37939
(865) 558-3595; www.americaoutdoors.org

American Whitewater
1430 Fenwick Lane
Silver Spring, MD 20910
(301) 589-9453; www.americanwhitewater.org

Professional Paddlesports Association
7432 Alban Station Boulevard, Suite B-244
Springfield, VA 22150
(703) 451-3864; www.propaddle.com

Trade Association of Paddlesports
P.O. Box 84
Sedro Woolley, WA 98284
(360) 855-9434; www.gopaddle.com

United States Canoe Association
606 Ross Street
Middletown, OH 45044-5062
(513) 422-3739; www.uscanoe.org

U.S.A. Canoe and Kayak
230 South Tryon Street, Suite 220
Charlotte, NC 28202
(704) 348-4330; www.usack.org

The following organizations provide general information on boating safety:

United States Coast Guard—Office of Boating Safety
www.uscgboating.org

United States Coast Guard Auxiliary
www.cgaux.org

National Association of State Boating Law Administrators
www.nasbla.org

National Safe Boating Council
www.safeboatingcouncil.org

United States Army Corps of Engineers
www.usace.army.mil

How to Be Safe on the Water

Anne and Gavin love to watch kayaking on TV adventure shows, and are noticing plenty of car and vacation ads that feature kayaking. The sport looks like a lot of fun, both are strong swimmers, they love the water, and they decide to buy boats and start paddling. After a winter of cabin fever and lots of rain, a spring day dawns bright and clear. Anne and Gavin drive to the local discount store and begin their adventure by buying paddles, life jackets, swimsuits, and cool shades. Before heading off to grab a couple of kayaks, they pick up a couple of six-packs of beer.

The description above was compiled from actual accident reports. At the end of this chapter, you'll be given an opportunity to identify risk factors that the paddlers will likely encounter and to identify ways Anne and Gavin can minimize or eliminate each risk.

Identifying and Reducing Risk

Become a safe paddler by reducing potential risk. Weather, water conditions, wind, temperature, equipment, prior planning, group composition, and experience all play a part in the safe-boating formula. Accepting your limitations, as well as those of your gear, and exercising good judgment will improve your chances of having a safe experience. Understanding the following key points will reduce your chances of a mishap and increase your enjoyment.

Using Crucial Equipment Appropriately
Life Jackets

According to the United States Coast Guard, most paddlers who drown are not wearing life jackets! The American Canoe Association requires that life jackets be worn during its paddling programs. Many states have similar requirements, and the United States Coast Guard requires everyone under the age of 13 to wear a properly sized and fitted life jacket while on a boat. Life jackets provide buoyancy in the water and work best when fitted securely. Remember, life jackets are also called Personal Flotation Devices, or PFDs. Contact your state boating agency to learn about laws that require life jackets and other safety equipment to be carried on board a kayak. Be smart. Wear your life jacket.

Kayak Flotation

You need to wear a life jacket, and your boat needs extra flotation too! Even boats that are made of a buoyant material are difficult or impossible to rescue when full of water. Built-in waterproof compartments, foam blocks, or inflatable air bags are a must, and they must be securely attached to the boat. This extra flotation will help a swamped or capsized boat ride higher in the water, making rescue, emptying, and reentry much easier.

PFD

kayak float

Clothing

Dress for the water temperature, not the air temperature. A layering system of clothing is important—air trapped between layers is good insulation, and adding or removing a layer of clothing allows easy comfort adjustment. Cotton clothing is a poor choice except in extreme heat, as cotton holds moisture when wet and cools the body. Wool and synthetic pile are much better insulators, wet or dry, but need a windproof and waterproof outer layer to increase their effectiveness. Proper insulation on head, hands, and feet will increase paddler comfort in cold conditions. Extreme cold requires wet suits or synthetic insulation under dry suits. In addition to supplying crucial flotation when in the water, life jackets are also a valuable outside insulating layer

Footwear

Footwear is a critical item of paddling gear. This is not the time to go barefoot! Cuts to the feet and sprained ankles are the most common injuries among inexperienced paddlers. Whether carrying a kayak over rugged, wet, and slippery terrain, or launching in ankle-deep water, choose good foot support and protection. In cold water, prudent paddlers should wear neoprene booties or old athletic shoes with wool or synthetic socks.

Additional Gear

What you carry will depend on your trip's length, access to services, and group make-up. For longer trips, consider taking the following: water bottle, sunglasses, sunscreen, insect repellent, first-aid kit, toilet paper, compass and maps, sponge, bailer, whistle, flashlight, rescue rope and sling, knife, dry bags, extra paddle, matches, extra flotation for the kayak, duct tape, food, guide books, garbage bags, glasses straps, camera, fishing gear, and emergency signaling devices. Coast Guard regulations require anyone paddling on federally regulated water to carry a sounding device and a light. A bright flashlight and a whistle meet these requirements.

Preparing for Cold, Wind, and Waves
Cold—Hypothermia

Cold water can disable even the strongest of swimmers! Exposure to cold water can cause hypothermia, a condition that results in a lowering of your body's core temperature. Hypothermia develops when the body cannot produce enough heat to keep its temperature normal. As the body's temperature drops, visible symptoms appear: unclear thinking, uncontrollable shivering followed by difficulty speaking, muscular rigidity, loss of coordination, and eventually loss of consciousness, then death.

Prevention is the key. The best way to prevent hypothermia is to "Be Aware and Be Prepared!!" Wear proper clothing (see above) and a life jacket that fits! When the water temperature is 55° F or below, or when water and air temperatures combined don't add up to 120° F, wear a wet or dry suit. Look for weather changes constantly. Be prepared and act quickly.

paddling pants

paddling top

synthetic layer

booties

light/sound device

dry bag

Wind and Waves

Waves can be great fun, but can lead to swamping or a capsize. Wind produces waves on large bodies of water. Stay in protected waters unless you and your group can handle rough water and are prepared to rescue overturned boats. Wind may either blow you off your intended course or slow your progress, and sometimes these setbacks can have serious consequences. Large waves are often found in flooded rivers, too. Floods are no place for the beginner, and recreational kayaks are not designed for such demanding conditions.

Learning Critical Skills
Wet Exits

Kayaks of all types do turn over, and paddlers must be comfortable with exiting a capsized craft. Sit-on-tops and most inflatable kayaks are usually easy to get away from, but a boat with decks, in which the paddler sits down, can present some challenges. A calm motion of bending forward at the waist, placing one's hands on either side of the cockpit near the paddler's hips, and pushing the kayak toward one's feet will allow a paddler to safely exit even a tight cockpit. Leaning back while in the sitting position can make exiting much more difficult.

If a spray skirt (also called a spray deck) is used to keep splashed water or rain out of the cockpit, the paddler must practice removing the skirt and exiting the boat to ensure safety. Because many recreational kayaks have large cockpit openings, the skirts for those boats are quite large. Swimming with such a large amount of material around one's waist can be difficult, and should also be practiced. Wet exits are best learned and practiced with an instructor standing beside the paddler to provide assistance and feedback. Spray skirts should not be used unless such practice has taken place. Paddlers using spray skirts typically wear helmets while running rivers.

Balance

You can decrease the chance of a capsize by staying low in the boat and being flexible at your waist. Let the boat rock back and forth, and maintain balance by keeping your head and torso over the centerline of the kayak. If you sit stiffly upright, you raise your center of balance and you can capsize more easily. Maintain a comfortably erect posture and let your hips swing with the boat's movement.

River Reading

Moving water has awesome power. Smart paddlers understand and respect its strength. High and fast water levels caused by rain, snowmelt, and dam releases are no place to learn kayaking. Fast, powerful water can push you into hazardous situations such as downed trees or other obstructions. Learn to recognize and respect the dynamics of the river. Experienced river paddlers use specialized equipment and know how to "read the river," or analyze the surface current. This skill helps paddlers determine where to go and what to avoid. River reading opens the door to the fun of "river running" and playing in rapids.

Review

From the scenario on page 9, list the risk factors encountered by the kayakers. There are at least 10.

1. _____

2. _____

3. _____

4. _____

5. _____

6. _____

_____

Now list ways to minimize these risks.

1. _____

2. _____

3. _____

4. _____

5. _____

6. _____

_____

To further test your knowledge of kayak safety, answer the following questions

1. What is a good rule of thumb for determining when a wet or dry suit is needed?

_____

_____

_____

_____

_____

2. Describe criteria for dressing for a kayak trip.

_____

_____

_____

_____

3. List items appropriate to take on a kayak trip.

_____

_____

_____

_____

4. What is hypothermia? What are its early symptoms?

_____

_____

_____

_____

5. What is the leading factor in boating drownings?

_____

_____

_____

_____

6. What are the most-common kayak injuries?

_____

_____

_____

Kayaks and Paddles

Gavin and Anne have decent jobs, and during the long winter have saved quite a bit of money to spend on recreation. After purchasing their swimsuits, life jackets, and beer, they go shopping for boats. The sales clerk shows them some really nice long boats with plenty of bells and whistles like hatch covers, decktop bungee cords for holding spare clothes and snacks, rudders, and more stuff they can't figure out. And they come in lots of great colors! The sales clerk doesn't know much about kayaking and can't really answer most of Anne or Gavin's questions, but they are really eager to try paddling, so they each buy a boat in their favorite color.

Kayaks

There is a bewildering number of different kayak designs on the market. No single design will do everything well, so you need to determine how and where you expect to paddle. Instruction and seeking the opinions of experienced paddlers are very good ways to get information, as well as reading up on the sport (*Paddler* magazine is a great resource). Since there are so many different designs, not all terms apply to every boat. For instance, sit-on-top kayaks don't have cockpit rims, inflatables don't need supplemental flotation, and some boats do not have footbraces. The following section describes some design basics and introduces common terms.

Top View

1. **Stern.** The back portion of the boat.
2. **Cockpit.** The opening where you sit.
3. **Bow.** The front or forward part of the boat.
4. **Deck.** The top of the boat.
5. **Footbraces.** Pedals, walls, blocks, or ridges to rest your feet on. Often adjustable.
6. **Keel line.** A real or imaginary line from end to end down the center of the kayak.
7. **Seat.** Usually central if solo; if tandem, the bow seat is closer to the bow end.
8. **Backband**. A strap, pad, or foam block that supports the lower back.
9. **Cockpit rim.** Reinforced lip of the deck, surrounding the cockpit opening.

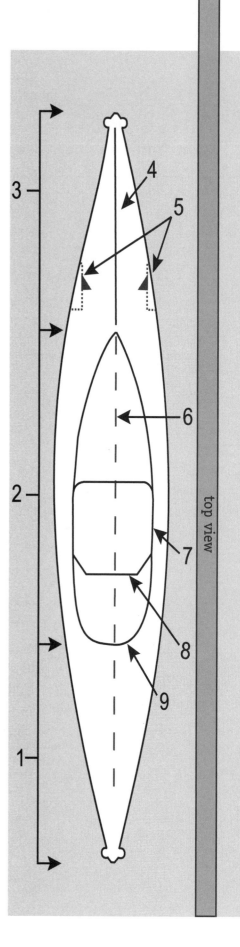

top view

side view

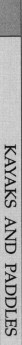

Side View

1. **Hull.** The body of the kayak.
2. **Cockpit rim.** Reinforced lip of the deck, surrounding the cockpit opening.
3. **Keel line.** The longitudinal centerline of the kayak.
4. **Backband.** A strap, pad, or foam block that supports the lower back.

Front View

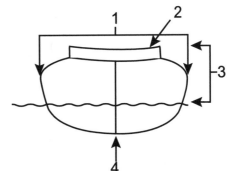

1. **Beam.** Width of the kayak at amidships.
2. **Cockpit rim.** Reinforced lip of the deck, surrounding the cockpit opening.
3. **Freeboard.** The vertical distance from the water surface to the lowest point along the side of the boat.
4. **Keel line.** The longitudinal center line of the kayak.

Selecting a Kayak

Select a kayak with volume appropriate to the weight to be carried. Remember that smaller kayaks are more efficient at moderate speeds. Kayaks designed for flatwater or ocean use tend to be long and lean with reduced rocker to enhance efficiency and tracking. Recreational kayaks need fuller lines and more rocker.

Kayaks are made from many materials, including animal skin and bone, wood, wood and fabric, aluminum and fabric, fiberglass, sandwiched plastic, and plastic and fabric composites. Individual preferences regarding tradition, ruggedness, lightness, performance, and cost all influence the selection of construction material.

Length is an important kayak measurement—it determines maximum speed and helps indicate capacity. Longer kayaks are faster than shorter ones, but the increased drag of the longer surface area requires more energy to achieve a given speed.

Width and fullness give an indication of forward efficiency, seaworthiness, and ability to travel straight or "track." Narrow, fine-lined kayaks are efficient trackers, requiring less effort at given speeds than wider boats. Narrow kayaks track well but are not as stable as wider models.

Cross-sectional shaping effects stability. Flat-bottomed hulls have good initial stability but roll badly in waves. Rounder bottoms are less stable when entered but more stable in heavy seas and generally track well. Flared hulls maximize seaworthiness by deflecting waves outward but make vertical paddle strokes more difficult for smaller paddlers.

Rocker is the upturn of the hull along the keel line. It affects maneuverability and handling. More rocker allows a kayak to be turned easily. Less rocker increases tracking ability but reduces turning ability.

Paddles

The boats were less expensive than they had expected, so Anne and Gavin decide to go for really good paddles. They find some exceptionally light short ones with bent shafts, again in sensational colors. These paddles cost more than the boats, but the product literature tag points out that the angled grips on the paddle shaft reduce strain on the wrists. When Gavin swings the paddle around in the store it feels great, like he could paddle all day with no problem! Two of the shortest, lightest paddles come in colors that really complement the two kayaks, so over to the cash register they go.

The paddle transfers effort into kayak movement. Proper paddle size and style increases the boat's responsiveness and makes kayaking more fun. Just as there are many options of size, shape, and material from which to select in boats, there are lots of choices in paddles. In general, a shorter paddle can more quickly perform maneuvering strokes, which are important for shorter boats in tight waterways. A longer paddle is better for straight ahead touring, particularly in long boats. A taller paddler can more comfortably use a longer paddle than a shorter person can. At the end of a long day on the water a paddler will appreciate a light paddle.

Kayak Paddle

1.   **Blade.** The flat section of the paddle which moves through the water.
2.   **Tip.** The extreme end of each blade.
3.   **Shaft.** The section of paddle between the blades.
4.   **Throat.** The junction between blade and shaft.
5.   **Powerface.** The side of the blade catching the water during a forward stroke.
6.   **Backface.** The other side of the blade.

Any length of paddle will probably work, but being comfortable and not having to do too much work can make the difference between a difficult experience and an enjoyable outing. Trying to use a long paddle in a tight stream can be frustrating, and having to frantically whip a short paddle back and forth to keep up with a group on open water is too much like work. A 190-cm paddle (6 ft. 3 in.) is on the short end of the spectrum. A 220-cm paddle (7 ft. 3 in.) is on the long end. Longer and shorter paddles can be found if needed, but most paddlers choose a length in between.

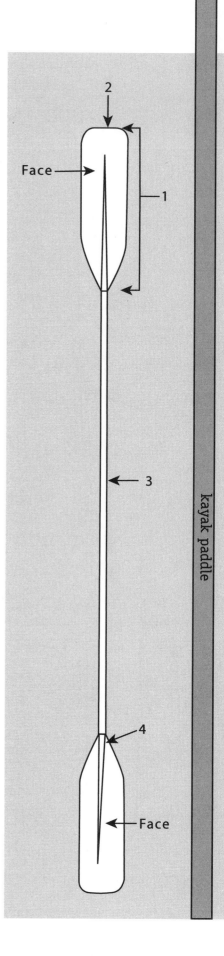

kayak paddle

Review

1. How do you measure for proper paddle length?

_____

_____

_____

2. How do you choose between shorter and longer paddles?

_____

_____

_____

3. Longer kayaks have the potential for greater _____ than shorter ones.

4. Describe how a river kayak should be shaped.

_____

_____

_____

5. Describe the performance differences between kayaks with round versus flat bottoms.

_____

_____

_____

_____

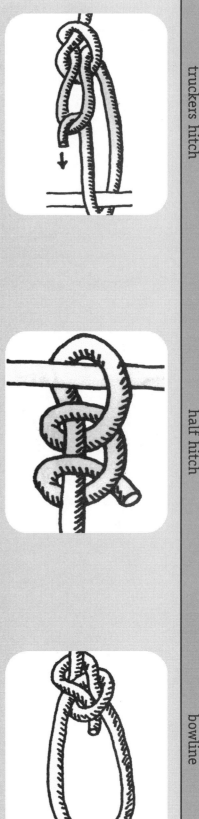

Getting the Kayak onto the River

Just getting to the river is an adventure. Gavin's kayak nearly flies off the roof rack of Anne's SUV when the hook on the end of a bungee cord pulls off, and both boats slide around some when they drive over 30 mph. But they finally arrive at a little park beside the river and carry the boats to the water's edge. Anne gets in her boat easily, but Gavin slips and falls in twice trying to sit down. Finally, tired from all the exertion, he just puts the kayak on the riverbank, and gets in. Then he pushes with his paddle and pulls against the ground to slide the boat into the river.

Tie Down

Kayaks should be secured amidships to cartop carriers (racks) and have both bow and stern tied to the vehicle's bumpers. Use two cross ropes or straps for the racks and kayak ends; secure ropes to bumpers or another solid part of your vehicle to form a ∨ (bumper to bow/stern to bumper). Make sure the racks are secure and both the vehicle and racks are sturdy enough for the load.

It is recommended that you use straps made of high-strength nylon webbing and strong buckles. If ropes are used, use proper knots such as the "truckers hitch," "half hitch," or "bowline." (See the ACA publication *Knots for Paddlers* for more information.)

Avoid the use of bungee or elastic cords. They may allow the boat to shift and fall off the car at highway speeds.

Lifting and Carrying the Kayak

Always lift a kayak using your legs to avoid back injury! Bend your knees to squat down beside the boat, roll the cockpit rim onto your shoulder, and straighten up carefully.

Lightweight solo kayaks can be carried short distances with the center point of the cockpit rim resting on a shoulder, the

supporting arm grasping the rim just in front of the shoulder for control.

Tandem boats, sit-on-tops, and heavier kayaks are carried more easily by two people. With a person on each end, kayaks can be carried by grasping beneath the boat's end, or by holding the grab handles.

Launch the kayak by placing one end into still water and "feeding" the boat hand over hand until it is floating fully. Do not let go of the boat!

Launching the Kayak

Launch the kayak and bring it parallel to the shore in water that is deep enough to float the boat when loaded. When on moving water, the upstream end needs to be held tight to shore, keeping the kayak from spinning into the current. In the shallows, the kayak is walked from shore into ankle-deep water. Always load cargo before paddlers. Trim the kayak level by equal load distribution.

Boarding the Kayak

To enter the kayak, lay the paddle across the boat behind the seat, with more paddle length toward shore. Facing forward, grasp the paddle with both hands behind you, and lean the kayak to shore until the paddle blade braces against the ground. Transfer your weight slowly onto the paddle and slide into the kayak's seat. The smaller the cockpit opening, the sooner you will have to bring your feet and legs into the front of the boat. In boats with very small cockpits you may have to sit on the deck behind the seat to put your legs in the boat first. Again, use the paddle to steady you. Maintain

three points of contact when boarding and moving about in a kayak. Either two hands and one foot, or both feet and one hand should be in contact with the craft at all times. Climb directly into your paddling position whenever possible.

Balance and Stability

For maximum stability, stay loose! Imagine hinging your body at the waist. Keep your upper body and head over the centerline of the boat as you swing your hips from side to side. Start off by tipping the boat just a little back and forth, side to side. Staying flexible as the boat moves in the water is the key to maintaining balance. Most kayaks are very stable as long as you keep your balance. Leaning out over the side of the boat with your upper body is an easy way to turn over. Foot braces improve stability and paddling efficiency. Push against the foot brace on the same side as your paddle stroke to get the best energy transfer.

When paddling tandem, the stern paddler generally enters the kayak first. The stern paddler can then easily view the bow paddler's entry and help to steady the boat.

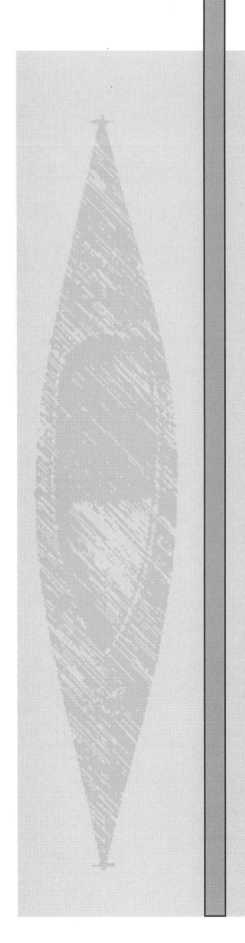

Review

1. Are bungee cords a good tool for securing your kayak to your vehicle? Why or why not?

_____

_____

_____

2. What muscles do the most work when picking up a kayak?

_____

_____

_____

_____

3. When boarding a kayak at the river bank, which end should be kept tight to shore?

_____

_____

_____

_____

4. You should keep how many points of contact when moving about on a kayak?

_____

5. What is the best way to maintain balance once you are seated in the kayak?

_____

_____

_____

_____

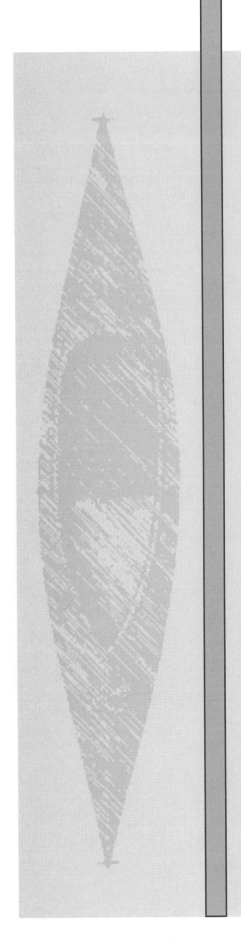

Kayaking Strokes

Paddling is the art of moving a kayak through the water. The key is to move your boat using maximum body and paddle efficiency. For best results, keep the paddle blade at right angles to the direction of travel; efficiency fades quickly as the angle changes. Keep the shaft vertical to the water surface when moving forward or in reverse. Keep the shaft horizontal on sweep strokes, which are used to turn the boat.

Holding the Paddle

When holding the paddle, space your hands apart a bit more than shoulder width. Sit up straight but twist your torso to reach as far forward as possible. As you move the boat by pulling your paddle against the water, use the large torso muscles to power the kayak. Your arms help with the stroke, but if you rely on just your arms you will tire more quickly.

Paddle Stroke Phases

Paddle strokes have three phases: catch, propulsion, and recovery. The paddle enters the water during the catch at right angles to the direction of travel or resistance. During the propulsion phase the kayak moves in a given direction. Recovery with a kayak paddle often means simply reaching forward with the other blade to start another catch. As the new blade moves into position for a catch, the first one comes up out of the water. Sometimes, as with sweeps or ruddering, successive strokes may be taken on the same side, with

the same blade. In this case the working blade is "recovered" to the starting position for repeating the stroke.

Stroke Terminology

Understanding the following terms will make the stroke descriptions more useful. Review the Glossary of Terms on pages 46–47 for more terms.

Working blade   The blade that is in the water, applying force.

Offset   This refers to the two blades of a kayak paddle not being in the same plane. Various offsets are used for different purposes. Having offset blades can reduce resistance on the nonworking blade as it moves through the air toward the next stroke. No offset, where the two blades line up with each other, is the simplest design.

Control hand   A paddle with offset blades needs to be twisted in between each stroke so that each catch can take place with the blade at 90 degrees to the direction of travel. This angle allows the blade to achieve the greatest possible resistance and increases efficiency. Only one hand is used to control this twisting, otherwise the paddler's wrists may be uncomfortable or even injured. Most modern paddles are right-hand controlled, which means the paddle shaft is held firmly by the right hand and twisted by that hand when necessary. The left hand loosely holds the shaft, allowing it to rotate as needed. This loose grip is important for avoiding wrist injury. In fact, a relaxed grip with both hands is safer and much less fatiguing. Left-hand-control paddles are available but can be hard to find.

Indexed grip   So that the paddler can orient the paddle blades without looking at them, the grip area on the shaft is an oval shape, or "indexed," designed to fit into the palm of your control hand. Some paddles don't have this feature, especially ones without offset blades.

The Strokes

While paddling strokes may be modified or combined to achieve the movement or reaction desired of the kayak, it is helpful to have a kayak paddle in your hands as you read the stroke descriptions that follow. All strokes can be practiced while sitting in a straight-backed chair.

The photos on pages 24 and 25 show solo paddlers, but all of the strokes can be adapted for tandem kayaking.

Because kayaks tend to turn under power, we first present turning and spinning strokes. These include the draw, sweep, and reverse sweep. Learning these strokes first will allow you to turn at will, and to stop turning at will, so you will be able to control your craft. Forward and reverse strokes are presented last.

Draw

The draw moves the kayak abeam (sideways) toward the paddle, or can turn the kayak when used at either end. The draw begins as the paddler twists to one side, aligning his or her shoulders with the centerline of the boat. The catch begins off the paddler's hip, with both arms extended and the paddle as vertical as possible. The blade is parallel to the keel line, the powerface toward the kayak.

The draw is powered by pulling the onside hip toward the paddle, keeping the top arm stiff and bending the bottom arm slightly. As the kayak approaches the blade, the power phase of the draw stroke ends. To recover, rotate the working blade so that you can slice the edge of the blade through the water to the catch position. Rotate the working blade back in line with the keel line to begin the next draw. This is an "in-water recovery."

Keep the paddle vertical in the water to increase efficiency. *Hint:* Moving the boat to the paddle creates the illusion of trying to pull water under the kayak. Think of your paddle as a broom that you are using to sweep dirt under a carpet!

Ruddering

Drawing in or pushing away with the paddle blade behind the paddler near the stern is called "ruddering" and is a useful steering technique once you have forward momentum. Body position is the same as for the draw, with the shoulders as nearly in line with the keel line as possible. The paddle is held fairly horizontally, with the working blade planted back near the stern, and on edge. With the blade fully immersed, push away or pull in toward the stern to steer. Keep the rearmost arm's elbow low, near the back deck. This will put less strain on the shoulder joint.

Bow Draws

Pushaways near the bow are rather awkward, but draws to the bow, or "bow draws," can be quite useful in certain situations, such as turning across eddy lines. Start in the same body position as for the draw, but with the paddle held on an angle with the working blade planted well forward and about two or three feet from the bow. Pull the bow toward the paddle, again using the torso muscles to power the stroke.

Forward Sweep

The forward sweep (also called simply "a sweep") turns the bow away from the working blade while maintaining forward momentum.

The paddle shaft is held horizontally during the forward sweep. The paddler leans forward slightly, rotating the torso 45 degrees toward the direction the boat is to turn (the working blade's arm and shoulder reaches forward). At the catch, the paddle blade is on edge in the water alongside the bow. Using torso rotation to power the stroke, the blade arcs in a wide semicircle to the stern. Watch the paddle blade as it moves through the semicircle to help

draw

ruddering

bow draw

forward sweep

reverse sweep

forward stroke

back stroke

generate torso motion. Extend both arms to arc the paddle out as far away from the boat as possible without compromising balance, with both hands eventually out over the water. The shaft arm should bend slightly only as the blade nears the stern. Bending the arm at this point is important to protect the shoulder from potential injury.

If another sweep is needed, return the paddle from the stroke's end to the catch position and repeat.

Reverse Sweep

The reverse sweep turns the kayak sharply toward the working blade, reducing forward momentum.

The paddler's body rotates toward the direction you want the boat to turn, with the working blade planted close beside the stern, and on edge. The paddle shaft is held horizontally. The arm closest to the stern is slightly bent (elbow down) with the hand well behind the paddler's hip. With the paddler looking at the blade, the torso uncoils, arcing the blade out away from the boat and forward, and pushing the blade's backface against the water. The bow swings toward the stroke with the stern swinging away. Recover by twisting back to the plant position if another reverse sweep is needed.

The solo paddler's sweep arcs 180 degrees and travels from "tip to tip," or end to end, of the kayak. In a tandem kayak the team performs sweeps together, on the same side of the boat. Care and communication are needed to keep from banging paddles, but nearly full sweep strokes are still possible.

Forward Stroke

The forward stroke moves the kayak forward and is the key to successful paddling. A stroke on one side of the boat will turn the boat away from that stroke. The further out the paddle arcs away from the boat, the more the boat will turn. Alternating strokes from side to side will correct that veer, but for increased efficiency keep the forward stroke parallel to the keel line, as close to the boat as possible, and relatively short to keep the blade vertical through the power phase.

Reach as far forward as you can without leaning, then twist your torso to reach even further. Twisting allows you to use large muscle groups in your torso, and leaning forward prevents effective twisting. Plant the paddle so that the entire blade is in the water. Allow your torso to "untwist" back to a neutral position, using those torso muscles along with your arm to pull against the paddle. Imagine pulling the boat forward past the paddle, remembering to keep the blade as close as possible to the boat. Lift the working blade out of the water when it is near your hip and reach forward with the other blade for the next stroke. Taking the stroke farther back wastes energy by lifting water and turning the kayak.

Back Stroke

The back stroke is used to stop forward motion or to move the kayak backwards.

This stroke is simply the forward stroke done in reverse. Slice the blade into the water near your hip and push it forward until it comes out of the water near your bow. Keep the blade close to the boat, and alternate sides as you would with a forward stroke. Twisting your torso into this stroke will give you more power, but since most folks find backing up quite challenging, more power may not be a good idea. This stroke (done slowly with correct form) is good for warming up shoulder muscles, and frequent practice will really improve your overall boat control.

Maneuvers

When you perform a stroke, it seems that the paddle is moving relative to you and the boat. Of course, the object is for the boat to move. The movements of the boat on the water, including spins, turns, ferries, moving abeam, and many more, are called maneuvers. First a few very simple maneuvers are covered, then dynamic maneuvers used on rivers are discussed.

Spins

Spins rotate the boat on its center. Solo kayaks spin easily with sweeps or reverse sweeps. Tandem kayaks can spin with several mixtures of bow and stern strokes. In tandem boats with seating positions close to each other, you must take care not to whack your partner with the paddle on these combined strokes. The two working blades will be on opposite sides of the boat, and the nonworking end of the paddle can get in the way. A few combinations are:

➤ A bow reverse sweep and stern sweep.
➤ A bow sweep and stern reverse sweep.
➤ A bow draw in unison with a stern draw.
➤ A bow pushaway in unison with a stern pushaway.
➤ A bow cross draw in unison with a pushaway.

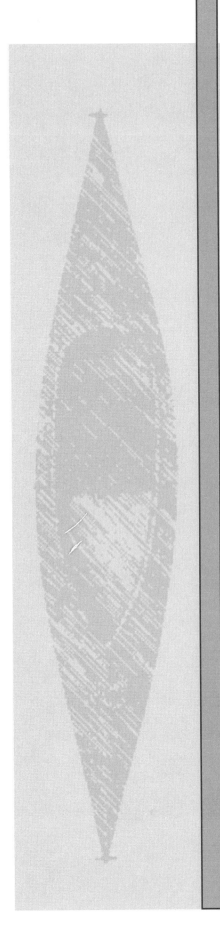

Turns

To turn the kayak while moving, select strokes that reduce drag. While a variety of strokes may turn the kayak, the following combinations are most effective at maintaining forward momentum:

➤ Turn solo kayaks using a draw stroke to the bow, or a sweep.
➤ Turn tandem kayaks by combining a bow draw with a stern sweep.

Moving Sideways (Abeam)

This maneuver moves the kayak sideways without turning it. Moving abeam is useful for leaving and approaching shore and avoiding obstacles in moving water. Draws and pushaways move the boat abeam. Pushaways are particularly useful when bringing a boat to shore or to a dock. As the kayak gets close to shore, there may not be enough distance or depth to properly perform a draw, so a pushaway on the side away from shore is the stroke of choice.

Paddling a Double or "Tandem" Kayak

Tandem paddlers work together as a team. The bow paddler sets the cadence; the stern reads and follows the bow's lead. The bow, however, should feel the rhythm of strokes and listen for instructions from the stern. Bow and stern paddle on the same side of the boat, in unison. This keeps the paddles from banging into each other and lessens the chance of one paddler accidentally hitting the other. Remember, it takes time, patience, and lots of communication to build a tandem team.

Review

1. What is the proper hand positioning on the paddle?

_____

_____

2. Why are feathered recoveries important (see the Glossary of Terms for help with this one)?

_____

_____

3. Name three key points about tandem paddling.

_____

_____

_____

4. Why keep the paddle shaft vertical on draws, pushaways, forward, and back strokes?

_____

_____

5. Why do we hold the shaft nearly horizontal for sweeps and reverse sweeps?

_____

_____

6. What phase of the paddle stroke transfers the most force to the water?

_____

_____

Kayaking on Moving Water

Anne and Gavin float comfortably along and enjoy the scenery for quite a while after getting on the river. The boats move along well, and just a few backstrokes on one side or the other keep the boats pointed downstream. Anne notices some rocks ahead and tells Gavin that the current seems to be speeding up. Gavin sees a wide gap between rocks and tells Anne they should paddle toward it. They have a hard time keeping on course, with the kayaks swinging from side to side. They make it through the gap, and the water speeds up in earnest. They see a sharp turn to the left, but the current pushes them to the right. Anne is very uncomfortable and feels out of control. She yells to Gavin that they should go to shore, and he agrees. But they take off toward opposite shores!

Strokes and maneuvers executed and developed on flatwater provide an excellent foundation for paddling on moving water. In addition to basic strokes, you need to understand river dynamics and how to "read" the river. You also should understand the force of moving water. A gallon of water weighs about eight pounds. The faster water flows, the greater kinetic energy, or force, it creates. Hundreds, even thousands, of pounds of force can be created against a pinned or trapped person or boat.

Understanding the characteristics of the moving-water environment allows you to develop understanding and respect. Take a river paddling course to learn about moving water before venturing out.

How to Read a River

Downstream V

A downstream V is a surface feature of the river formed by two parallel obstructions, indicating a clear, deep water path.

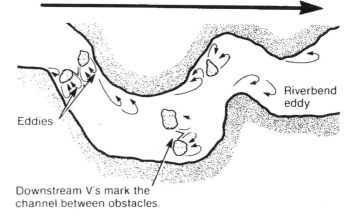

CURRENT DIRECTION

Eddies

Riverbend eddy

Downstream V's mark the channel between obstacles.

Water lines formed off the obstructions join downstream, thus pointing the way.

Standing Waves

Standing waves are formed usually at the base of a drop or down-stream ∨ caused by accelerating water coming in contact with slower moving water downstream. Standing waves are a series of waves that are stationary, but the water is moving. Big waves are sometimes referred to as "haystacks."

Eddy

An eddy is an obstruction, usually above the water's surface, that forces moving water to go around it. As the downstream flow of water fills in behind the obstruction, it creates an upstream, relatively slow movement of the water, called an eddy. Eddies provide stopping spots for paddlers to rest and look downstream.

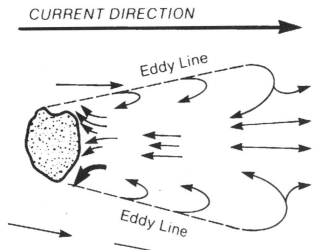

Eddy Line

An eddy line is the border between the eddy current and main current flow, distinguishing a change of current direction.

Pillow

A pillow is a smooth, shallow mound of moving water covering a structure just below the surface. The mound of water is not sufficiently deep to paddle over. A white wave or depression just down-stream is a clue of trouble upstream. Remember, in river paddling, "pillows are stuffed with rocks."

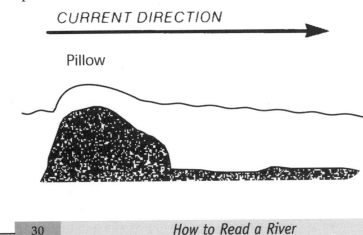

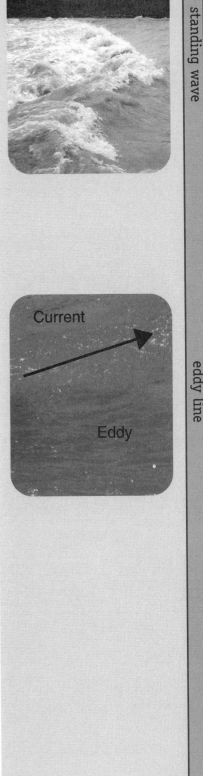

standing wave

eddy line

Hole

A hole is a depression in the river's surface caused by water flowing over a rock or ledge.

River Hazards

Hydraulic

Water flowing over an obstacle and landing on surface water below creates a depression. Downstream surface water rushes upstream to fill in this depression creating a vertical whirlpool effect. When the hydraulic is large enough to trap and recirculate a boat, it is referred to as a "keeper."

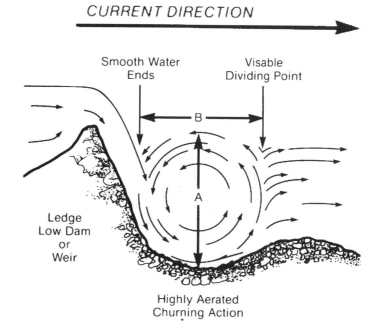

CURRENT DIRECTION

Smooth Water Ends

Visable Dividing Point

B

A

Ledge Low Dam or Weir

Highly Aerated Churning Action

Low-head Dam

A low-head dam is a manmade river hazard and is difficult to detect from upstream. It can be recognized by a horizontal line across the river called a "horizon line." These structures can create keeper hydraulics, which are difficult to escape. Low-head dams are often called "drowning machines." All dams should be portaged.

High Water

High water is another term for flood. Moving water has awesome power, especially at high water. Learn river reading and moving-water maneuvers before you go out. Look for tell-tale signs of high water, and avoid paddling rivers when these signs are present. They include: muddy or discolored water, water above normal banks, possibly flowing through brush or trees that are typically dry, lots of garbage, trees, etc., being carried along by fast agitated water. These conditions can be life-threatening! Know your limits and use good judgment. Choose to paddle when conditions are more manageable.

Strainer

Strainers are obstacles in the river such as trees, cables, fences, brush, drainage grates—anything that can trap debris while allowing water to pass through. The force of moving water can pin people and kayaks against strainers, leading to serious injury and even death. Avoid strainers at all costs! Never underestimate the danger.

Broaching

A broach occurs when the current pushes a boat sideways against an immovable object causing the boat to stall or stop. To guard against broaching, lean the boat toward the object. Leaning toward the rock or obstruction allows upstream water to flow under the boat, "lifting" it around the obstruction and potential danger.

River Maneuvers

Paddlers use specific maneuvers to get around on moving water. Because of the remarkable forces created by moving water, the paddler's strength is no match. Instead, learn to harness the power of the river. Learn to finesse the river with efficient river maneuvers like the ones listed below.

Ferrying

Ferrying is a method of crossing current without getting swept downstream. The ferry uses the water's energy deflected off the side of the kayak. This force, balanced against upstream paddling, results in lateral movement of the boat across the current. Ferrying is helpful to line up for running downstream Vs, or for maneuvering around hazards like rocks and strainers.

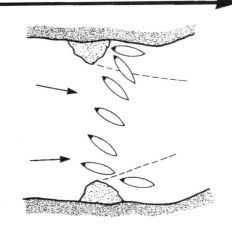

CURRENT DIRECTION

The key to successful ferrying is in both boat angle and speed. The slower the current, the greater the angle to that current. To ferry, point the upstream end of the kayak slightly toward the shore you wish to reach and, holding that angle, paddle upstream into the current. Continue paddling until you reach the other side.

There are upstream and downstream ferries. Typically, the easiest ferry is the upstream, or forward power and sweep ferry. The bow of the kayak is pointed upstream, and the paddler primarily

uses forward strokes and stern draws. This makes it easier to see the current and make adjustments for a successful ferry. In tandem kayaks, the bow paddler provides power while the stern paddler is chiefly responsible for angle and direction.

For the downstream or back ferry, the bow of the kayak points downstream, and the paddler primarily uses back strokes. This allows the paddler to better see where the kayak is going or what it is avoiding. In tandem kayaks, the stern paddler provides power while the bow paddler is chiefly responsible for angle and direction. Solo or tandem, this is typically a more difficult maneuver to execute.

Navigating Bends

Flowing water will try to go in a straight line. When geography forces a river to turn or "bend," the water will push to the outside of the curve and current will be fastest there. This fast current tends to wash away the outside bank of the river, and any trees or rocks on the bank will fall into the water, forming strainers and obstructions. These serious hazards can be most easily avoided by staying on the inside of the bend. If there are any obstructions on the inside of the bend, the current will assist the paddler by helping to push the boat to the outside. More typically the hazards will be on the outside, so plan on the inside route.

Eddy Turn

Boat speed, boat angle, and boat lean (heeling) are key components to entering an eddy. Enter the eddy with enough speed to cross the eddy line, but not so much that you fly out the other side. Approach the eddy so you will enter it at about a 45-degree angle. Lean the kayak just like leaning a bicycle through a turn. Boat lean will stop your boat from capsizing to the outside of the turn as the boat enters the slower-moving, upstream-flowing eddy.

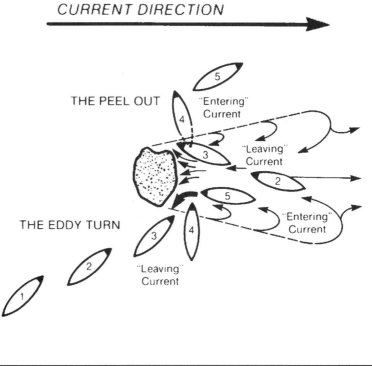

CURRENT DIRECTION

THE PEEL OUT

THE EDDY TURN

Peelout

A peelout is fast, exciting, and sometimes the only way to exit an eddy. Just like the eddy turn coming in, boat speed, boat angle, and boat lean are key components to the peelout. Exit the eddy with enough speed to cross the eddy line. Go too slow, and you may not be able to cross the eddy line. Cross the eddy line with an angle similar to the one used in the ferry maneuver, again depending on the speed of the mainstream current; the faster the current, the closer to pointing directly upstream you should be. Another useful visualization is to imagine yourself on a giant clock-face, with 12 o'clock directly upstream, and 6 o'clock directly downstream. Ninety degrees would correspond to either 9 or 3 o'clock; 45 degrees would be half way back toward upstream, or 10:30, or 1:30, depending on which side you need to turn to. Unless the current is very slow, you will probably cross the eddy line pointing at around 11 or 1 o'clock. Lean the kayak just like leaning a bicycle through a turn. Boat lean resists capsizing upstream as the boat enters the faster downstream-moving current. And you'll be more stable if you continue paddling throughout the turn.

Review

1. Why is a river like a book?

2. What are three common factors in eddy turns and peelouts?

3. Why should you avoid low-head dams?

4. Name and explain three river hazards.

5. What force aids in ferrying a boat?

6. Which is more difficult, an upstream or a downstream ferry?

A Sample River

Know your put-in and take-out before you begin. Travel in groups of at least three boats. Keep the boat behind you in sight. The lead boat should be able to recognize and avoid hazards: low-head dams, high rapids.

Upstream Vs indicate rocks

The river is usually faster on the outside of a bend. When you approach obstructions, set your course in advance, using good ferry angles. When in doubt, scout from the shore and walk around (portage).

Trees and other objects in the river are potential strainers. Steer clear of them.

LOOK OUT! If the river disappears, you may be approaching a steep drop or water-fall. Scout and portage. Run only if properly trained and equipped, using all precautions.

If capsized, stay on the upstream side of the kayak. Keep your feet up. Never stand in moving water unless it is less than knee deep. Set a res-cue point with a knowledge-able paddler on shore before running any difficult drop. If you are not prepared to swim the rapid, don't paddle it!

Portage Route→

1. Preferred Course

2. Riskier Course— current is faster and likelihood of being swept into a strainer (if present) is greater.

Rescue and Safety

Anne hits a large wave and tips over with her boat sideways in the current. Gavin hurries over to help. The coldness of the water shocks Anne. She floats well in her life jacket, with her head clear of the surface, but the cold has her gasping for air. Gavin paddles up beside her, and she grabs his boat. She tries to hold on to her own boat and paddle. Her kayak is floating nose down with the stern nearly straight up in the air, so it is really hard to manage. She lets go of her boat, but holds onto her paddle as Gavin pulls her to shore. At the riverbank Anne, cold and tired, pulls herself out of the water. Gavin makes sure she is up on dry ground and then hurries downstream to see if he can find her boat.

Rescue

Capsizing is part of the sport of paddling. Boaters should be able to handle their own craft in capsizes or swamps and aid others in need. Whether assisting others or saving yourself, remember that people come first! You may need to let of a boat or other gear if you are being swept toward a hazard. Always be prepared to swim. Dress properly and wear your life jacket. Being prepared is the first step to rescue. Remember, any rescue will be safer and easier if the boat has adequate flotation. This means having inflated air bags, foam blocks, or waterproof compartments in the boat. Without this supplemental flotation some boats may be impossible to rescue.

self rescue

Self-Rescue

Self-rescue is often the quickest and surest way to deal with a capsize. The simplest self-rescue is to wade or swim to the closest safe shore with the kayak. In moving water, stay on the upstream side of the boat; this prevents entrapment of your body between the kayak and downstream obstructions. On a lake, if the self-rescue involves a long swim, you may want to reenter the boat even if it is partially flooded. Whenever possible, stay with the boat. It provides positive flotation, and a large object is more visible to rescuers as well as to powerboats that might otherwise not see you.

In moving-water mishaps, it may be best to release the kayak and swim to shore. The safest method of swimming in moving water is on your back, with head up and feet pointing downstream with toes at the water's surface. Use your feet to fend off rocks. Position your body to ferry into the nearest eddy, using strong kicks and your arms to help direct your movement. Do not stand up in the current until you are in water less than knee deep. Standing in moving water that is more than knee deep may result in injury or drowning due to foot entrapment.

avoid foot entrapment

Emptying the Kayak

To empty a capsized boat floating in shallow water where you can stand near shore, turn the boat so that it points toward the shore.

Push down on the end of the boat that is away from shore and push the other end up onto the land. With the kayak still upside down, raise the end that is away from shore so that the water drains out. A kayak full of water is very heavy, so keep your knees bent, back straight, and get help, if possible, to avoid back injury. After allowing several seconds for the boat to drain, roll the kayak to the upright position on the surface of the water. In deeper water, a boat-over-boat rescue is most effective (see p. 39).

Reentering the Kayak in Deep Water

If shore access is not possible, you can reenter the kayak from deep water. One method is to crawl up on top of the boat from the stern with your legs straddling the boat. Bring your legs forward and slide into the seat when you reach it. If your boat is very wide (beamy) you can enter from the side. Begin by placing your hands

on both sides of the cockpit rim near the wide section of the kayak, although hand placement may vary due to kayak width and stability, arm length, and paddler strength. There should be space available for your body inside the open cockpit. Pressing down with both hands and using a strong kick, lift the body upwards until the hips are across the near side. Roll onto your back and sit inside the kayak before bringing in your legs. Balancing the boat during these maneuvers is difficult and requires practice. A second boat can assist by holding the cockpit rim or side opposite the side being reentered,

continued on p. 39

Reach—Throw—Row—Go

Reach

First reach with your voice. A call or a whistle blast to get the victim's attention is a good idea. Often, reaching a hand to a swimming paddler can bring him or her safely to shore or to your boat. A paddle can extend your reach safely.

Throw

When the swimmer is too far away to reach with a paddle or pole, a thrown float or rope can often aid in the paddler's rescue.

Row

If the swimmer is beyond range of a thrown rescue device, the rescuer should maneuver his or her boat closer so that a reach or throw technique is possible. A rescuer in a boat is safer than a swimming one.

Go

As a last option, a trained and properly equipped rescuer can swim to the aid of the swimmer. Bystanders should call for help.

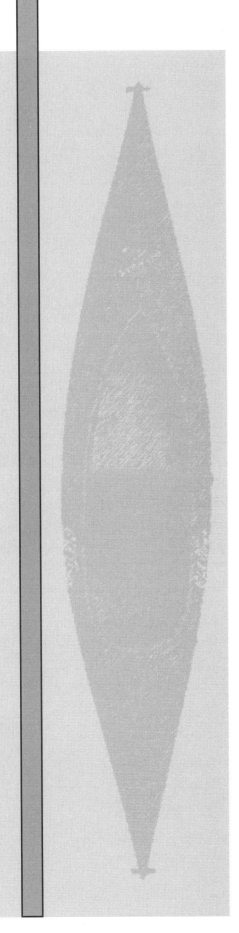

stabilizing the boat. Tandem paddlers help stabilize the boat for their partners and reenter one at a time. Accessories such as paddle floats, sponsons, or a rescue sling can help you get back in your boat, but no matter the technique or gear you rely on, practice is key.

After reentry, hand-paddle the boat, if necessary, to retrieve paddles and gear. Swamped kayaks may be paddled to shore with paddles, or if necessary with your hands. They may also be bailed or pumped dry. Carrying a bail bucket or pump is an important part of being properly prepared.

Rescuing Others

When in position to assist others, use this rescue sequence: Reach—Throw—Row—Go. See facing page.

Bulldozer Rescue

When paddling to rescue a swimmer, tow the swimmer at the stern of your kayak while bumping the swamped boat to calm water at a close shore.

Boat-over-Boat Rescue

In open water with a second kayak to assist as a rescue boat, a boat-over-boat rescue is quick and very effective. Assume a kayak has capsized:

The capsized boater helps line the capsized boat up perpendicular to the rescue boat forming a T, and remains in the position at the bottom of the T. The rescuer at the top of the T holds onto the capsized boat's end, allowing the capsized boater to push down

on the away end of the boat, raising the near end up and out of the water. Keeping the boat upside down, the rescuer pulls the boat up and across their craft until it balances on their boat forming a +. Be careful not to pinch fingers between the two boats. The capsized paddler should keep hold of the upside-down kayak as it is pulled up and over, then move to a stabilizing position on the end of the rescue boat. The rescuer allows the boat to drain, then flips it upright while continuing to balance it across their own boat. The rescuer slides the kayak into the water without losing contact. The two boats are then held side to side while the swimmer reenters the boat.

Remember that any of these techniques may be impossible unless the boat is equipped with supplemental flotation. Whatever type—air bags, foam, or watertight compartments—added flotation should be inspected and maintained regularly.

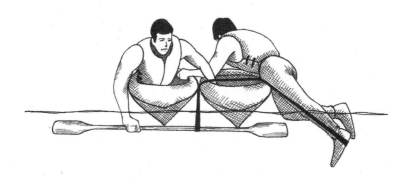

Rescue Sling

A method that enables a paddler to climb into a boat with little difficulty is the rescue-sling technique. Loop over the side of the swimmer's boat a section of line or webbing long enough to hang into the water. Place the loop across the boat onto a second boat, or onto a paddle placed crossways beneath both boats. If a second paddler is in the water to help stabilize, secure the loop directly around the cockpit rim or around the hull of the boat being entered. The paddler then places a foot in the loop, using it like a stirrup. Lifting the hips above the top of the cockpit, the paddler climbs into the center of the boat.

Exposure in Water

When paddlers are unable to reenter their craft quickly, they may risk hypothermia, especially if water or air temperature is low. The Heat Escape Lessening Posture (HELP) and HUDDLE position minimize heat loss in cold water.

The HELP Position

The HELP position protects the highest heat-loss areas of the body: the head, neck, underarms, and groin area. This technique is possible only when wearing a life jacket. To adopt the HELP position, the individual swimmer:

➤ Crosses the legs at the ankles and pulls the legs toward the chest;
➤ Crosses the arms at the chest being careful to protect the area under the arms, or holds the neck with the hands for additional protection;
➤ Keeps the head out of the water.

The Huddle

A group of paddlers huddling together conserves body temperature more efficiently than floating alone. To HUDDLE, body-to-body contact is critical. Form a circle, placing smaller or weaker individuals inside. Wrap arms around one another with legs together.

Review

1. Name the steps in the rescue sequence.

2. Why stay with the kayak when capsized or swamped?

3. Why is it hazardous to stand in moving water?

4. Describe two techniques for minimizing heat loss in cold water.

5. What could Anne have done to make her kayak easier to rescue when she swam?

6. What should Gavin do after he has towed Anne to shore?

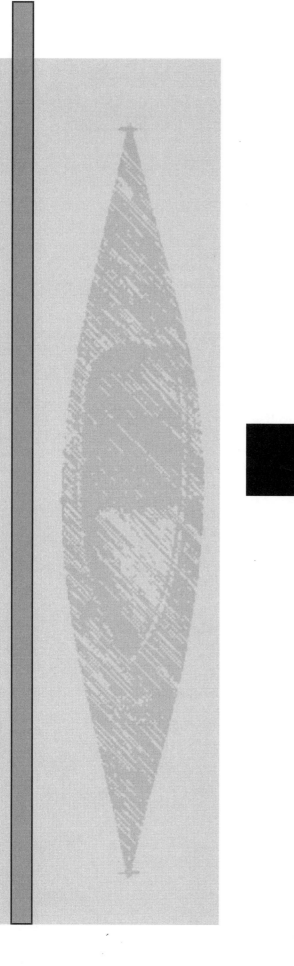

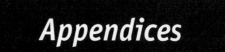
Appendices

American Whitewater River Classification

Class I—Easy. Occasional small riffles consisting of low, regular wave patterns. About what you might encounter on a lake on a mildly windy day.

Class II—Medium difficulty. Rapids occur more frequently, usually retaining a regular wave pattern as on a lake with a fairly vigorous wind (enough to cause whitecaps). Although there may be more than one route, the most practical one is easily determined. There may be simple, uncomplicated chutes over ledge up to three feet high.

Class III—Difficult. Numerous rapids, with higher, irregular standing waves, hydraulics, and eddies. In Class III rapids you must maneuver. The most practical route may not be obvious, and you'll find that you have to work a little. Expect ledges up to four feet, waves up to three feet, overhanging branches, and deeper water.

Class IV—More difficult. Long, extensive stretches of rapids with high, irregular standing waves and difficult hydraulics, holes, eddies, and crosscurrents. Good boat control is essential, and you are working very hard. Class IV requires plenty of fast decision making, because the most practical route may not be obvious. Difficult ledges with irregular passages, "stopper" waves, or souse holes may block the way.

Class V—Extremely difficult. It's not always easy to tell where Class IV ends and Class V begins. These rapids are not only difficult but they are long and continuous. Irregular stoppers and souse holes are unavoidable; partially submerged boulders and ledges are everywhere; very complex eddies and crosscurrents are not only present but occur in long, dazzling combinations. Common usage also refers to short, very intense rapids as Class V if they require a lot of skill and courage to run.

Class VI—Utmost difficulty. This isn't a hard class to define, but in recent years there's been a tendency to ignore the definition. It's supposed to mean the utmost limit of navigability, with its chief distinguishing characteristic being unusual risk of life. Mistakes made here can be fatal. No one should ever be urged or taunted into running a Class VI rapid.

When the difficulty of a river falls between two grades, two numbers will be used: Class II–III. If most of the river is of one classification except for one or two spots, it is referred to as, say, Class III(IV). These ratings are for normal water levels, and classifications may change drastically in high water. Similarly, river ratings usually drop about a class in low water. If you run a few Class IVs in low-water conditions, don't assume you are a Class IV paddler.

American Whitewater
1430 Fenwick Lane
Silver Spring, MD 20910
(301) 589-9453
www.americanwhitewater.org

Waterway Security

WARNING!

Do not approach within 100 yards of any U.S. naval vessel. If you need to pass within 100 yards of a U.S. naval vessel in order to ensure a safe passage in accordance with the Navigation Rules, you must contact the U.S. naval vessel or the Coast Guard escort vessel on VHF-FM channel 16.

You must operate at minimum speed within 500 yards of any U.S. naval vessel and proceed as directed by the Commanding Officer or the official patrol.

Violations of the Naval Vessel Protection Zone are a felony offense, punishable by up to 6 years in prison and/or up to $250,000 in fines.

Because of Homeland Security concerns, many Federal properties now have security zones. Naval vessel protection zones direct boaters to stay at least 100 yards away from all large naval vessels (unless directed to approach) as well as installations, piers, and other security zones. Make sure you know about local restrictions, too. Help keep America safe.

Kayaking on Lakes and State Waterways

Many lakes and rivers are marked with information and regulatory signs and buoys indicating restricted or hazardous areas. It's important to keep in mind that not all hazards are marked. The safe paddler always obeys these signs:

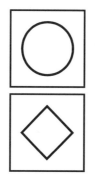

Controlled Area.
Look in the circle for further information. These are found at speed zones, no fishing areas, no anchoring areas, ski zones, no wake zones, etc.

Danger—Use Caution.
This may mark construction areas, reefs, shoals, or sunken objects.

Boats Keep Out.
The nature of the danger may be placed around the outside of the crossed diamond. These may mark waterfalls, dams, swim areas, or rapids.

Information.
These tell directions, distances, and other non-regulatory messages.

Glossary of Terms

Abeam: At a right angle to the keel line.
Afloat: On the water.
Aft: A term describing direction toward the rear or stern of a boat.
Aground: Touching bottom.
Amidship: Describing the midsection of a vessel.
Astern: Aft or toward the stern.

Backband (back rest): Provides support for the lower back while kayaking and helps with erect posture in the boat. Located behind the seat, and usually made of padded fabric, plastic, or foam.
Backface: The side of the paddle blade opposite the powerface.
Beam: Vessel's width amidship.
Blade: The broad part at the ends of the paddle.
Boil: A mound of water deflected up by underwater obstructions.
Bow: The forward end of the boat.
Bracing stroke: Used to help a paddler regain balance. Can be dangerous if performed with poor technique, for this reason it is considered a more advanced stroke, requiring personal instruction.
Broach: To be turned broadside by wind, wave, or current.
Bulkhead: A cross-sectional wall inside a kayak, made of composite, plastic, or foam. Bulkheads provide structural support and, if sealed around the inside of the hull, can create watertight compartments for buoyancy and storage. They are sometimes also used as foot braces.

Capsize: To turn the kayak over in the water.
Catch: The part of a paddle stroke placing the blade in the water.
Channel: A route through obstructions in a section of river.
Chine: The transition from hull sidewall to bottom.
Chute: A narrow channel between obstructions with fast water.
Control hand: Hand used to twist the paddle shaft so as to use offset blades.
Cockpit: The enclosed central compartment on a kayak, in which the paddler sits.

Deck: The top part of a kayak that keeps the hull from filling with water.
Difficulty Rating: The rating of a river section's navigability.
Downstream V: Formed when there are two obstructions and water passes between both to form a V which points downstream.
Draft: The depth of water a kayak draws.
Drop: A steep sudden slope in a river; often called a rapid.
Eddy: The area behind an obstruction in current with still water or upstream current.
Eddy line: The line that separates the eddy from the main current.

Falls: Drops where water falls free.
Feather: To move the paddle by leading with one edge, thus reducing the drag caused by air or water during recovery phase.
Ferry: Maneuver in which a paddler uses the force of the water to move the kayak sideways across the current.
Flatwater: Lake or river water without rapids.
Flotation: Waterproof compartments, foam blocks, or inflatable air bags. This flotation will help a swamped boat stay on the surface, making rescue and reentry easier.
Foot pegs (foot braces): Usually adjustable structures inside the cockpit on which a kayaker places the balls of his/her feet. See "Bulkhead."

Haystack: Standing waves below a chute where water flow slows.
Hull: The structural body of the boat, the shape of which determines how the boat will perform.
Hydraulic: Turbulence caused by water flowing over an obstacle.

Hypothermia: Physical condition that occurs when the body loses heat faster than it can produce it.

Keel: The longitudinal centerline of the kayak.
Keeper: A hydraulic that holds objects in recirculating water.

Ledge: A projecting rock layer partially damming water flow.
Low-head dam: A fixed obstruction across a stream or river in which water drops over the crest creating a hydraulic that can trap and recirculate objects.

Peelout: Turning downstream from an eddy.
PFD: Personal flotation device. Cushions, and most importantly for kayakers, life jackets. PFDs used in the United States must be U.S. Coast Guard approved and must be worn to be effective. The Coast Guard recognizes five types of PFDs. These must be used in accordance with the label. Kayakers most commonly use Type IIIs.
Pillow: A boil where water deflects upwards from an obstruction.
Powerface: The face of the blade that pushes against the water on the forward stroke.

Rapids: River section with steep fast flow around obstructions.
Recovery: Moving the paddle from stroke end to the next catch.
Riffles: Water flow across shallows causing small waves.
River left: The left side of the river as you face downstream.
River right: The right side of the river as you face downstream.
Rocker: The amount of curvature of a line down the middle of a kayak's hull, from bow to stern. More rocker (more curvature) usually makes a kayak more maneuverable. Less rocker tends to help the kayak track in a straight line.
Roll: The technique of righting a capsized kayak with the paddler remaining in the paddling position.
Rudder stroke: A stern pry or draw to control direction.

Shaft: The long skinny part of a kayak paddle.
Sit-on-top: Kayaks without a cockpit, sit-on-tops are usually self-bailing with various seat and foot brace configurations. Many are for recreational use, but some are designed for touring or racing.
Slack water: Water flowing without riffles or rapids.
Slice: Edgewise movement of the paddle blade through water.
Spray skirt (spray deck): A neoprene or nylon skirt worn by a kayaker that attaches to the rim (coaming) of the cockpit. It keeps water out of the kayak.
Standing wave: A wave occurring where current decelerates, also called a haystack.
Stern: The rear end of the kayak.
Stopper: A hydraulic that arrests forward momentum.
Stow: To secure gear in a boat.
Strainer: An obstruction in moving water which allows water to pass through but stops and hold objects such as boats and people. Fallen trees often form strainers in current.
Swamp: To fill (a kayak) with water.
Sweep boat: The assigned last kayak in a group of paddlers.

Thigh braces (knee braces): Usually found in whitewater and touring kayaks, these structures inside the cockpit give the paddler points of contact important for boat control.
Tip: The extreme end of the paddle blade, or alternatively, to turn a boat over.
Throat: The transitional area where paddle blade and shaft meet.
Trim: The bow-to-stern leveling of a kayak that affects boat control. In most cases it should be nearly level, or with the stern slightly lower in the water.
Trip leader: An experienced and qualified paddler leading the group on an outing.
Trough: The depression between waves.

Upstream V: Formed by an obstruction in current which creates a V that points upstream.

Waterline: The intersection of hull and water surface.
Wet exit: Coming out of a capsized kayak.
Whitewater: Aerated rapids.